A Journey from Shame to New Life

One woman's story of alcoholism

Catherine Jenkins, CSJ

For copies of A Journey from Shame to New Life contact:

Good Ground Press
1884 Randolph Avenue
St. Paul, MN 55105

Phone: 800-232-5533 or goodgroundpress.com

Cover Design: Ansgar Holmberg, CSJ

ISBN-13: 978-1978242708
ISBN-10: 1978242700

Copyright © 2017 by Catherine Jenkins. All rights reserved. Printed in the U.S.A. Material in this book may not be reproduced in whole or in part in any form or format without special permission from the publisher.

Introduction

A number of years ago, I had an article published in Review for Religious (November/December 1989) in which I explored the possibility of an unbreakable thread of spirituality that ran through my life. The spiritual lifeline began when I was a very small child and persisted, as I grew older, through about twenty-one years of ever worsening secret alcoholism. I firmly believe and cherish this as an integral part of my life.

    As I approach my ninety-fourth birthday, I want to record my experiences and feelings as I expressed them in my journal during those dark months of the last years of my active alcoholism. In April 1979, I attended an Intensive Journal Workshop and continued to journal almost daily after that. Perhaps my experience can help another person, particularly another woman, caught in the seemingly helpless struggle with alcoholism—the fear of failure, of hopelessness, and of being found out.

Catherine Jenkins, CSJ

☙

From 1941 through 1980 I was a member of a cloistered religious community for women. After Vatican II, some monasteries began to place more emphasis on the contemplative aspect of the life, which demanded education, and less on the strictly cloistered aspect. I was blessed to have been able to further my education in scripture, theology, and philosophy during those years. Unfortunately, I was also able to get out and obtain alcohol.

In 1980, due to circumstances which may not be so prevalent now as they were years ago, when most women religious knew very little about alcoholism, I made the painful decision to leave a contemplative lifestyle for an apostolic one. However, I am convinced that whether I had entered a cloistered way of life, an apostolic community, or had married or lived a single life in the world, I'd have become an alcoholic. My lifestyle had nothing to do with it. Often when I have shared my story, I have said that I am very fond of baked potatoes but I cannot remember when I tasted my first one. However, the three times I had alcohol before I entered the convent at eighteen remain vivid. I loved the taste as well as the effect.

My first encounter with alcohol occurred when I was seven or eight. My mother asked me to wash the pantry shelves. I climbed up on a stepstool and lifted the rarely used dishes from the top shelf. Among them was an attractive glass bottle containing a dark red liquid. I removed the glass stopper and sniffed the contents. The fragrance was delicious, so I tasted it—wonderful! A few days later, I found my parents standing in the kitchen puzzling over the bottle my mother held as she told my dad that the contents were diminishing. I sailed in and settled their curiosity by saying, "I'm drinking that, Mama! I like it!" The bottle disappeared.

The second occasion occurred in 1933, the year prohibition was abolished. That summer Dad made grape wine and proudly presented it for Christmas when several of our Connelly relatives gathered for dinner. Each one received a small glass full. I downed mine in one swallow, pronounced it, "Good, Daddy! I'd like some more!" I did not receive it.

After graduation from high school in 1941, I had my third and last encounter with alcohol before I entered the convent. Two of my older cousins treated me to lunch. I have no recollection of the food, but we each had a Tom Collins beforehand—another red-letter day!

☙

On September 15, 1941, I entered the Poor Clare Monastery in Sauk Rapids, Minnesota, and began a new way of life. We arose early and retired early. Our days were filled with prayer and manual labor. That fall we laid a sidewalk. In the spring we built a retaining wall. Each Sister had a vegetable garden and a flower garden to care for. Our reading matter consisted of biographies of the saints and what I came to think of as "fervorino"—books which aroused our emotions. Due to our active outdoor work and the fact that we were blessed with an abbess who possessed a remarkable amount of common sense, we were spared many of the psychological problems in some cloistered monasteries. However, when I was in my early twenties, I remember being disturbed by how childish, not "childlike," I had become. I longed for intellectual stimulation. On April 22, 1942, I became a novice, "Sister Mary Michael of the Holy Trinity."

☙

In 1953 our monastery had nearly reached its capacity, and we did not want to become larger. Sister Anne Condon had dreamed for several years of founding a new monastery in or near Minneapolis. On the feast of Saint Clare in 1952, she petitioned Bishop Peter Bartholome of St. Cloud for permission to explore possibilities. By the early spring of 1953, five of us had volunteered and been accepted to form the new community. Our average age was twenty-six. In St. Paul, Archbishop John Gregory Murray gave his approval to the venture. In April, Sister Anne and I made our first trip out of enclosure to view an offered site that proved to be unsuitable. In May, a parishioner of St. Richard's in Richfield, Minnesota, alerted Father Alfred Longley about our search for land suitable for a monastery in the area and he announced it at Mass. Mrs. Marie St. Martin immediately offered five acres of her large farm before she sold it to a realty company for development. The property had been an asparagus farm with sandy soil and not a tree in sight, but we saw possibilities and happily accepted it.

We made numerous train trips to the Twin Cities to confer with the Archbishop, Catholic Aid, Father Longley, benefactors, and architects. The Sisters in Sauk Rapids gave what they could to help us financially. Bishop Bartholome made a large loan with no interest. After many adventures and misadventures, our little community prepared to move permanently to the St. Paul - Minneapolis Archdiocese in November 1953. The Sisters of St. Joseph of Carondelet offered us hospitality at the Academy of the Holy Angels in Richfield, close to the site of the monastery. Other communities of Sisters hosted us for numerous meals, which forged enduring bonds among us.

The original monastery building was what we called the "basic unit." It would house twelve nuns with a small cloister chapel, an extern chapel, a small novitiate room, kitchen, library, dining area, and two dormitories, one for the Sisters in final vows and one for girls who had recently entered, novices, and temporary professed young women.

In late spring, our money was running out. Every morning we left Holy Angels after early Mass and breakfast to work on the interior of the monastery. We taped the joints on the sheetrock between rooms, applied the preliminary coat of whitewash, and painted the interior walls except for the chapel and bathrooms. Other Sisters came to help us. Numerous other people helped in many ways. By August 12, 1954, on the day of the feast of St. Clare, we had moved from Holy Angels to live and work at the monastery located in Bloomington. We had been in a community of twenty-six in Sauk Rapids and lived among many Sisters of St. Joseph at Holy Angels. Now we were only six and had to get used to life with each other as a community. Many curious visitors came through each day. This continued until late October when Archbishop John Gregory Murray officially enclosed the monastery.

Because we did not have enough finally professed nuns to hold an election, Archbishop Murray appointed Mother Anne as Abbess and me as her Vicaress. Mother Anne immediately named me as Novice Mistress, too. Within a week a young woman joined us and we were seven! Our numbers grew rapidly. By 1957, we had to build an addition to the monastery.

☙

During these years in our Bloomington monastery, I was blessed with closer contact with my parents. Several years before, in 1946, Dad had begun to have unusual episodes. He acted in strange ways or fell on the floor in seizures. Most of the time he was lucid and was the strong, gentle, loving father I had always known. However, these periods, which the doctors weren't able to diagnose at the time, were the source of deep concern to him, my mother, my brothers, and me. One day he came to see me, visibly shaken after he had to commit his aunt to a mental hospital. He said, "I'd rather die than have to be in a place like that." I told him, and I firmly believed it, "Dad, God won't let that happen to you. You are so good."

In 1957, following several bizarre incidents after which Dad was confined to the psychiatric floor at Anker Hospital, a hearing was held at which Dad was present. He remembered nothing of what he had done, but he responded, "If I have done these things, I need to be committed. It's not safe for me to be at home." Mom signed the papers; otherwise the state would have committed him. She told me it would have been easier to sign his death certificate. He was taken to Hastings State Mental Hospital. I was shaken to the core. Sometime in the night, I went to chapel and sobbed dry sobs.

It was a painful maturing in faith. I began to realize that I could not set limits to faith. While God did not cause bad things to happen, the world and all of us are imperfect and evolving. I did not then, nor do I now, believe God was testing. I grew to believe that "in the end all will be well." God is one with us in all that we go through. In the words of Beatrice Bruteau, when we have exhausted all that we can say about our "descriptive selves," we are left with "I am." We are one with God; God is one with each of us. I believe Jesus tried during his life to make us understand that. I believe the beautiful creation myth in Genesis tells us that truth. God breathed into the clay and the human came to life. If God withdrew His breath from us we wouldn't be. This faith developed over the years, faintly during the years of my active alcoholism, and then deeply and firmly during my recovery.

☙

Looking back, I believe I became an alcoholic in 1958. As Vicaress I had keys and access to any wine or brandy that we received. I knew nothing about alcoholism, but I had developed a craving for liquor and would do nearly anything to obtain it.

In panic, I tried what I later learned is called a "geographical cure." In April 1959, I returned to our founding monastery in Sauk Rapids, Minnesota. The decision to return was made without any counsel or dialogue, simply out of terrible fear and deep shame. On New Year's Day, in inner turmoil, I wrote this poem:

The Circumcision, 1958

My soul is flat on its face, small Christ,
Beneath all incensed words, all rose-hued singing.
Past even the scalding brine of tears,
In sere vigil to the rough wood clinging.

If gift this be, small Christ,
This pain-racked peace past singing,
Breathe the spilled torrent of Your Love
Into these dry bones, to the rough wood clinging.

My soul is flat on its face, small Christ,
Blind to the plaster Babe, deaf to the caroled singing,
Locked in the first red rush of your pity,
Spiked to the Form on the rough wood clinging.

Because of my shame, I could not share my addiction with anyone. Our cloistered community in Bloomington had grown from six women to eighteen; several were still in the novitiate, but I walked out. The next couple of years were, quite simply, a nightmare in spite of the fact that our Sisters in Sauk Rapids had lovingly received me back. Almost immediately I knew I had made a terrible mistake in leaving the group I helped found. I missed the Sisters in Bloomington, especially those in the novitiate, as well as the courses in systematic and mystical theology and scripture taught mainly by our Brother Franciscans from their newly opened seminary in Chaska, Minnesota.

For several months I did not drink. Then in the fall I was appointed infirmarian. Once again I had access to the keys to the cupboard next to the Abbess' office where gifts of wine and brandy were kept.

A few months after my return, my father, who had spent two and a half years in a mental hospital, was released to go home on medication. Two months later my mother died, and Dad soon quit taking his medication. In May 1960, under very painful circumstances, he was returned to the hospital where he died one year after my mother. Since our rules were strict, I was unable to be with my parents or family. Other women religious had experienced the pain of enclosure and had gracefully accepted it, but I numbed my feelings with alcohol, and my drinking increased.

As infirmarian, I slept in the infirmary and was not obliged to get up for the Divine Office at midnight. After the Sisters had gone to chapel, I often crept upstairs to the Abbess' office, took the keys to the cupboard where wine and brandy were kept, and quietly returned to my space between the two infirmary rooms. As no one else was interested in opening that cupboard, my raids went unnoticed. Somehow, I still performed my duties as infirmarian. Both Sisters confined to the infirmary were content with my ministrations, as was our doctor. However, my conscience was not at peace. I thought drinking to excess was a sin. Each week I resolved to tell it in Confession, and each week I was unable to do so because of intense shame. Week after week I'd decide not to drink and imagine going to Confession and telling the priest "I used to drink." Of course that day never arrived.

As I look back now, I am amazed that for several years I continued to perform my duties as infirmarian. I prepared special meals for those on diets and cooked for our guests and for our chaplain who lived in a house just below the monastery. After one of our organists became crippled with rheumatoid arthritis, I was asked to play the organ. This made me very nervous, but I did it. To fortify myself, I secretly had a glass of wine before Mass each time I played.

☙

Vatican II thrilled me. I wrote two or three articles that were published in periodicals for women religious and priests. The Bishop and our chaplain were furious with me for an article in which I expressed the possibility of a change in the rules of enclosure. However, the Abbess was supportive and allowed me to write.

It is painful to write of those years when my emotions were so raw and carefully concealed under a calm exterior and quieted with alcohol. I loved the two Sisters in the infirmary, both original members of the founding community in Sauk Rapids.

One Sister was among the most genuine characters with whom I have ever lived. She was full of love and exasperating wiles. One day she remarked to me that when she wanted something from a Sister, "I can be very 'coaxy'!" She marched to her own inner drumbeat.

When she died in December 1963, it was with deep emotion I prepared her body for the undertaker. That day I mourned the loss of an original and independent but deeply human and loving spirit from our midst.

I told Mother Teresa that we could not send the usual short notice of her death to our Sister monasteries. This was not only because of her life in the monastery, but also because of the nearly unbelievable adventures with the original group of Sisters who were out of enclosure and going about the country collecting money to build a new Poor Clare monastery in Sauk Rapids in the early 1920s. Mother Teresa agreed and told me to write it. A few years later on the occasion of the Golden Jubilee of founding the monastery, I discovered that the piece I wrote had become a chapter in the Jubilee booklet created by a priest from the St. Cloud diocese. The opening paragraph stated that the article "was written by an unknown nun."

The other Sister died a few months later at the St. Cloud Hospital. During the months that followed, I spent many afternoons praying and writing in the sun-filled infirmary room with a view of our lovely grounds, lawns, and gardens.

During this time, two incidents occurred, both of which are vivid in my memory. One afternoon a young Sister in temporary profession came in, pulled up a chair in front of me, and said, "How do you stand it?" She was referring to the lack of intellectual stimulation in our community. I, too, was troubled by this, but my feelings of being unworthy, due to my secret alcoholism, made me uncomfortable being honest. I responded that I didn't have a problem with our situation. She looked at me and replied, "I don't believe you," then walked out. A short time after that, she left the monastery.

On another day, a very quiet, serious, and gentle Sister came in, began to cry and asked, "Sister Michael, aren't you drinking too much wine?" Of course, I hotly denied it and she left in tears. Years later I was blessed with the opportunity to make amends to her.

In the 1950s, Pope Pius XII called for monasteries of contemplative nuns to form federations so that the nuns could be enriched by mutual contact and assistance. By the 1960s, the Mother Bentivoglio Federation (among others) was formed. The Abbess of the New Orleans monastery was chosen as Abbess of the Federation. She had the right to visit the member monasteries and to speak with any Sister who wished to see her.

In 1967, she and Mother Anne of the Bloomington monastery arranged with the Franciscans who ran the College of St. Teresa in Winona, Minnesota, to offer a program of enrichment for Poor Clares. It was envisioned as a one- or two-year program offering classes in theology, scripture, art, and music appreciation. Permission was sought from Rome, but no response was received. Finally, with advice from a canon lawyer, the program opened in August 1967, with nuns from several other Orders, as well as Poor Clares, in attendance. They lived in a section of Assisi Hall, the home of the Franciscan second year novices and the junior professed. In the beginning, all the classes were taught there, so the Sisters could observe a form of enclosure. Mother Anne was named as Coordinator.

When Mother Francis Clare visited our monastery in Sauk Rapids, I told her of my intense desire to be a part of the program. For me it was a dream come true, an opportunity to engage in study with other like-minded women who shared a contemplative lifestyle. Certainly, somewhere in my sub-conscious was the belief that this would take care of my drinking. Strangely enough, it did not occur to me that my alcoholism had begun when I had ample opportunities to study in our Bloomington monastery.

The Abbess in Sauk Rapids and the other Sisters genuinely believed that this new venture was foreign to our form of life and were truly horrified that I wanted to be a part of it. Mother Francis Clare encouraged me to transfer to her monastery so that I could attend the program. Now, looking back after the passing of many years, I can understand the dismay of our community and the anger of the Bishop. Fourteen years earlier I had been part of the group leaving to found a new Poor Clare monastery, less than six years later, I had returned to Sauk Rapids, and now I petitioned to leave once more. I was caught up in a time of turmoil in religious life and in the world. I felt grief at the pain I was causing the Abbess who had always been my friend, but I felt I was dying inside. Unrecognized was the basic part alcohol played in it—and had for many years. Finally, in September 1967, Bishop Bartholome told Mother Teresa to let me go. I was on the move again, this time to New Orleans.

☙

Years later someone remarked that leaving contemplative religious life for an apostolic way of life must have been a great shock. No, the shock had occurred years earlier when I moved from a strictly enclosed way of life to a monastery in the throes of experimentation. Some Sisters still wore the traditional habit, but the majority wore an attractive tent dress and veil—brown, blue, maroon or green! We went out to classes, did our own shopping, attended special events, visited our families once a year and accompanied visiting Sisters and family members to the French Quarter. I soon learned how to take city buses (which later enabled me to get out and buy wine in supermarkets and drugstores).

Sisters from other monasteries were drawn to New Orleans. Some stayed; others returned to their home monasteries. Along with two Sisters in the process of transferring from another monastery, I was immediately sent with the Novice Mistress to attend formation workshops each month. The workshops drew Sisters, Priests, and Brothers from many communities in the Archdiocese. The Sisters Council and a psychiatrist from De Paul Mental Hospital sponsored the workshops. Mainly, they comprised fresh insights from Vatican II documents and sound mental health practices. I loved them!

For two months I did not abuse alcohol. Then on Thanksgiving Day, we had wine for dinner. I felt very lonely that day. In the afternoon, I went downstairs to the kitchen and took the leftover wine to my room. In tears, I sat on my bed and finished the wine. My alcoholism was active again, but at that time I was still able to hide it.

In Sauk Rapids, each month Mother Teresa had given me the checks signed by her, which I made out and mailed to various companies from which we had purchased items. Because of that, Mother Francis Clare thought I had been the bursar. Nothing could have been further from the truth! I had always loved English and writing, but math was my nemesis. I remember one very amusing incident. As Poor Clares, we depended heavily on alms for our day-to-day living. Nevertheless, we received many requests for money, which were put, in my mail box. One day I opened one from Planned Parenthood signed by James Michener. I showed it to Mother Francis Clare and asked how I should respond. She replied I should tell him we could not send money but that individually, each of us was doing all she could to keep the population down!

In January 1968, when I had been in the monastery for only four months of the trial period for Sisters who had transferred from another monastery, the novice director and several novices walked out. Two novices and one postulant remained. The Abbess and her council met and named me as Novice Mistress. I could never get Mother Francis Clare to sit down with me and discuss my appointment, so I could not be sure if it was a temporary situation or not. Perhaps because of my canonical status in the community, she didn't know. The two novices were truly beautiful young women, one black and one white, and they welcomed me warmly. A few months later, I had the painful task of dismissing the postulant. Most of the Sisters were shocked, and I felt very much alone. However, one Sister told me she had not been blind to what had been going on, and she wanted me to know she understood. I felt truly grateful for the words of support.

☙

In light of Vatican II, I thought it would be beneficial to the novices if we could all attend theology and scripture classes at Notre Dame Seminary in New Orleans. Mother Francis Clare agreed and told me to call and ask if we might participate. The answer was: "No. No women could attend classes." When I shared the news with the novices, Veronica, our black Sister, strongly urged me to call Xavier University, the only black Catholic University in the United States. I thought it an excellent suggestion. The university's response was very positive; we were welcomed as students.

Since Charlene, the other novice, had attended a year of college before she entered the Poor Clares, she was in a second year theology class. In one class, I was the only white person. During the next semester, I took a sociology class with many black students and only two other white students, both from Pennsylvania. On the Louisiana Avenue bus, I was often the only white person. It was a real education for me. It was 1969. Black people were rising up and demanding their equality, but New Orleans was relatively peaceful.

One day during the summer, the novices, the postulant, and I went with another Sister to dig young trees from the property of a relative of one of the older Sisters. We planned to transplant them into our yard in New Orleans. After a couple of hours of hard work, she invited us in for a cold drink before we left for home. As we sat in her living room, she regaled us with stories of the "drunken nigger" who had once worked for her. I felt outrage and wanted to leave immediately. As we left, the woman embraced each of us or so I thought. The following morning, our postulant came to my office and told me that as I had walked out first, I had not seen what happened. Instead of embracing Veronica, she turned away from her and embraced the postulant who was white. I was horrified! "Veronica won't tell you," she said, "but I think you ought to know." I thanked her and told her we would never return to that house.

A few minutes later, when Veronica came to my office, I told her I had learned of what happened and that we were not going back. Then I held up her very refined, lovely mother as an example for her and told her that the woman who had given us the trees was ignorant. She stood for this for a minute or so, and then she erupted. "Oh, yes," she said, "it's so easy for you to sit there and say those pious things! You're not black! You don't know what it's like to be black!" She screamed at me for several minutes and then stormed out. I was shaking, for in those days novices didn't scream at their directors. I was shaken to the core. I went down to the chapel and sat alone to calm down. I thought, "She's right! I don't know what it's like to be black!"

Later, I shared the incident with Bishop Perry, the Auxiliary Bishop of New Orleans, who was also black. He related racial incidents that had happened to him as Bishop. A few weeks after this painful time, both Veronica and Charlene were scheduled to make their first profession of vows. Veronica came to me and asked if she could go to a black hairdresser and have her hair straightened as many young black women were doing that year. As we had not begun to go to beauty parlors, I told her I'd have to ask the Abbess. Mother Francis Clare willingly gave the permission. When I told Veronica, she threw her arms around me and asked, "Will you go with me?" That was the most healing response she could have given me.

☙

In the summer of 1969, during a Catechetical Pastoral Institute (CPI) class in Christology at Notre Dame Seminary, I had an experience that changed my thinking about the afterlife, especially the meaning of "purgatory." In the midst of class, I suddenly had an experience of being caught up into Christ. It was intense, more feeling than vision. I felt myself being embraced and gazed upon by a loving presence with eyes of fire, but not a painful fire, rather a gaze of love. I also experienced a feeling of sorrow. But more than any other feeling, I felt intensely loved. It is impossible to express what I felt. I have no idea how long it lasted before I found myself sitting in class. The feeling continued to overwhelm me for a long time. I partially shared it with only a couple of people. In my long life, I never experienced anything comparable. Even recalling it now fills me with awe. I believe it was a mystical experience, which through the years kept weaving the thread that has formed my thinking about the Holy. It has persisted through painful periods as well as through banalities and deep joy.

☙

In the summer of 1969, no one had applied to enter our community, thus I had no novices to work with. I reminded Mother Francis Clare that she had promised that I might attend the program at St. Teresa's in Winona, Minnesota. She agreed, and I was blissfully happy. Shortly after that, I went down the basement to get some canned goods for our dinner and experienced a sudden, extremely sharp pain in my foot. By afternoon my foot was terribly swollen. I couldn't wear my shoe. Our doctor came that day to see one of our older Sisters. Mother had him look at my by then grotesquely enlarged and painful foot. He sent me immediately to an orthopedic surgeon who took x-rays, discovering that the joints were horribly jagged with arthritis. He couldn't understand how I had been walking on it.

I had been born with both feet clubbed in an era when often little could be done. However, a Sister at St. Joseph's Hospital in St. Paul gave my parents the name of a fine orthopedic surgeon who put my feet in casts when I was three weeks old. The casts were changed periodically. My mother said I learned to walk in them. As a result I had no major problems in walking or running. I could not ice skate and, to my sorrow when I was thirteen; I could not take ballet lessons. However, those were minor inconveniences even if I didn't think so at thirteen.

But now in 1969, to see if fusing the joints would remedy the problem, the doctor put me in a walking cast for a few weeks. It proved to be the answer. I had no pain. He wanted to operate that summer. But I was going to St. Teresa's and I feared the opportunity, so long desired, might not come again. I told him (to his astonishment) that I wanted to wait until after my return in late spring of 1970. So off I went on crutches and wearing a triple "e" wide slipper on my swollen foot.

My dream had come true! In high school, I took only electives in which I knew I could do well. Now I took everything I could and thoroughly enjoyed every minute. My alcoholism became less active because I simply could not obtain alcohol except when we had it for special occasions.

In the spring, the night before our final exam, I suffered a major seizure. To this day I don't know if it was from alcohol withdrawal, as I had had no access to large amounts of alcohol, or from severe hypoglycemia, which was later diagnosed. Sisters Anne and Charlene, my companion from New Orleans, accompanied me to the Winona hospital where the doctor recommended that I be anointed, as I was totally unresponsive. Sister Charlene said that as soon as the anointing was over, I began to regain consciousness. My recollection is that I came to with an indescribable sense of peace. The priest's head was all that was visible, like the "Cheshire Cat," and I repeated again and again, "Thank you, Father!" A couple of days later, we returned to New Orleans by train; from Chicago we traveled in a sleeper car. I felt extremely weak but confident I'd be back in Winona in August.

About three weeks later, in June, I had surgery. When I awoke, I was amazed to have a heavy cast from my hip to my toes! That cast remained on until the end of September. Then, since my heel had not yet fused, I had a knee-high cast for two more months. There would be no return to St. Teresa's that year. In March 1971,

I finally completed therapy and was able once more to walk unaided. I haven't much recollection of how much I drank. I do remember one day when everyone was in the chapel, I somehow made my way to the infirmary room where Sister Marie, our nurse, kept brandy. I sneaked a glass-full back to my room.

☙

That summer I met a Jesuit from Loyola who became one of our chaplains offering daily Mass for us. Ben soon became one of my closest friends, the first close friendship I had ever had with a male.

In the spring of 1971, two unexpected requests were made of me. The Archdiocese had become concerned about another cloistered group of women in New Orleans. Bishop Perry asked me to work out a program of education for them with scripture, theology, and health-related classes for the fall of 1971 and the winter and spring of 1972.

Sister Fara Impastato, O.P., who was active on the Sisters' Council and taught scripture and theology at Loyola University, had become a close and dear friend. She agreed to teach. The administrator of Mercy Hospital agreed to give classes in health and nutrition. A Prioress was brought from another monastery to enable the Sisters to make needed changes. I know others also agreed to teach classes, but after all these years, I cannot remember their names.

Periodically, I visited the Prioress, but I never entered the enclosure. When I was at St. Teresa's, Fara visited them for me. At the end of the year, some of the younger Sisters transferred to other monasteries and older Sisters moved from the large, old monastery to a smaller home. In 1998, I attended an Elderhostel at a Benedictine monastery in Louisiana. There I learned to my utter surprise that the former Prioress and other Sisters (at least one from another monastery of their Order) were opening a new monastery nearby with the help of one of the Benedictine monks as their chaplain! The monk graciously offered to take me out to visit them. The elderly Prioress, now in a wheelchair, and another elderly nun came in to greet me accompanied by a younger nun. They remembered me and welcomed me warmly. At that time they were still living peacefully without enclosure. For me it was a joyful surprise as I had often wondered about them.

In the spring of 1971, another unexpected request came. Sister Anne had been Coordinator of the program for contemplative nuns at St. Teresa's since it opened in 1967. Now she had acquired nearly enough credits for a degree but needed to be relieved of her duties as Coordinator in order to devote to her studies fulltime. Sister Eunice, the Abbess of the Poor Clares in Omaha, had succeeded Sister Francis Clare as Federation Abbess. Sister Eunice asked me to take Anne's place.

I accepted with a joyful heart because it meant rejoining the program. However, I had some trepidation because Anne's place would be hard to fill.

Initially, Sister Eunice said I could take only one class as I was there primarily for the Sisters. Fortunately, the registrar convinced her I'd be "climbing walls in boredom," so she allowed me to take two classes. I chose another year of Greek and Philosophy 101, which I thought would be an introduction to Greek Philosophy, Plato, and Aristotle. Instead it was Thomas Dewey and American Philosophy. It turned out to be providential. Numerous footnotes referring to Alfred North Whitehead caught my attention and excited me because I was so interested in learning more about his philosophy.

The next semester, I took the first of my independent studies in process philosophy. The Sisters in the program that first year helped to make my year as Coordinator a good one. However, I was horrified when I heard one of my former novices contributing to a discussion of the other Sisters' novitiate experiences and attributed some comments to me. I exclaimed, "I never said that!"

"Oh, yes you did!" was the reply. As I looked back and pondered my early years as Novice Mistress, I realized I had been too strict out of sheer fear of not being "good enough" as if it had all been up to me. Privately, over time, I met with each of the first three who entered and apologized. It warmed my heart when one said, "You were strict, but I always knew you loved me." I have pondered that many times since and realized that genuine love may overcome mistakes. Throughout this year my drinking continued whenever I could go out and get wine, but it still remained a guilty secret.

Among the Franciscans who taught at the College of St. Teresa's, two stand out as having been an enormous blessing in my life, Sisters Emmanuel Collins and Helen Rolfson. Emmanuel lived in Assisi Hall. In addition to teaching us a class in literature, she gave lectures to the young Franciscan Sisters to which we Poor Clares were invited. She was a brilliant, warm, and truly beautiful woman, wise and humorous. Helen was young and also brilliant, fun loving, and creative. I took several independent studies in theology under her and she encouraged me to do things I never thought I could do. Sometimes on early mornings in spring, we biked out to the lake and prayed together as the sun rose, then returned to Assisi Hall in time for Mass. On the whole my years at St. Teresa's were fruitful and peaceful. In the summers I attended classes in New Orleans at Loyola and at CPI.

ଓଃ

My friendship with Ben Wren, S. J. continued and brought a great deal of beauty into my life. It was marred, as I realize now, by the fact that I felt I was a failure as a woman religious and a Poor Clare. Because of my closet alcoholism, I felt unworthy of his friendship.

Knowing I loved ballet, he took three of us to the Bolshoi when the Russian dance company came to New Orleans. In the summer of 1972, with Mother Francis Clare's permission, Ben took me and two other Sisters very early one morning to Dauphine Island off the coast of Alabama where he celebrated Mass among the sea oats. We had a picnic lunch and he introduced me "to our Sister the sea." This experience remains a lovely memory. At the time, it had a healing effect on me, as I felt depressed over the departure of two fine women, one a Sister of St. Joseph from New York who had entered our monastery two years previously. I thought the women had brought a degree of maturity to our community and was dismayed to see them go. Of course my closet alcoholism was not contributing to the health or maturity of our community's life.

In the early fall, I returned to St. Teresa's. There were more challenges in our group that year, which took more of my time. Nevertheless, I felt blessed to be there and thoroughly enjoyed my studies in process philosophy and New Testament Greek, especially St. John's Gospel.

My drinking had not yet reached the point where others were aware of it. I was forced to cut back since it was significantly more difficult to obtain alcohol, especially in the winter months. It was challenging to find a liquor store within walking distance of campus, but when I was able to get out and buy it, I did. I felt very foolish as I made up stories about what it was for. I can still see the amusement in the clerk's eyes as I explained to him that my sister had an extremely bad cold and I had heard that brandy would help. "Should I add it to tea or give it to her straight?" I asked. As I write this I realize I was buying brandy, not wine. Always in the back of my mind were the fear of being found out and the feeling of being a fraud.

In the spring Sister Anne graduated with a major in French, the first in our program to do so. In my coordinator position, I had let our Sisters go on campus and take part in the events that had previously been forbidden. Although Sister Anne was fearful that Rome might close us down, she never objected but supported my leadership.

One of the classes I took was a wonderful course on Philosophy and Literature at St. Mary's University in Winona. Our professor was a brilliant Jewish man who had lost his faith because of the Holocaust. For the works of modern literature we read, he gave us the underpinnings of philosophy. I had never really liked the

Book of Job, but when we read it as background for J. B. by Archibald MacLeish, our professor made it all come to life. I wrote a paper on it. The last sentence was: "In the end Job realized there were no answers, only communion." The paper received an A, but the professor left this note: "Communion with what, the Infinitely Malicious?" I felt profoundly sad.

ଓଃ

In February 1973, I had another seizure of short duration but which was extremely enervating. I went to the Mayo Clinic in Rochester for tests. The doctors couldn't find a reason for the seizure. Because further tests could be dangerous, they prescribed Dilantin and recommended an EEG after my return to New Orleans. At that time of year, with snow covering the ground, my drinking was comparatively light. After my return to New Orleans in the spring, my physician followed the recommendations from Mayo but eventually told me the EEG's had not shown any problems. He believed my seizures were caused by extreme hypoglycemia. A five-hour glucose test confirmed this and he put me on a low carbohydrate, sugar-free diet. He also wanted to take me off Dilantin, but I panicked at the thought and begged him to let me stay on it for a while. I would not eat a bite of anything containing sugar, and I stayed on Dilantin out of fear, but I drank wine with high sugar content.

My doctor's wife was an active member of Alcoholics Anonymous, but neither he nor any other physician asked me about my consumption of alcohol. Perhaps that has changed, but back then husbands and doctors too frequently would not allow themselves to believe a wife or a woman religious was an alcoholic.

Extreme tiredness followed this seizure. I chose not to do extra work needed in one class to obtain an A. I simply was not able to write a fine review of Whitehead's Science and the Modern World. I disappointed my professor as well as myself, but I never questioned my drinking as being a problem.

In the spring I made the decision not to return as the Coordinator in the fall. I needed to become a present member of our community in New Orleans. Sister Eunice was disappointed but she accepted my decision. Since there was not another Poor Clare able to fill the position, Sister Helen Rolfson, O.S.F., agreed to become the Coordinator. By that time, other monasteries had permission for their members to attend classes in their own areas. The need for a special program was no longer so important as it had initially been. Its purpose of opening the way for Sisters in contemplative communities to study had been remarkably successful.

One offer I regretfully refused came from the professor of the class on philosophy and literature I had been taking at St. Mary's University in Winona. He invited me to join a six-week seminar on Wittgenstein when school let out. I wanted to accept, but I knew that I needed to be back in our community in New Orleans. Sadly, I did not have the same insight about my alcoholism, but I continued to think I could do something about it with prayer and will power. I had no idea it was a disease.

That summer of 1973 remains something of a blur. I'm sure I attended classes at Loyola or the Catechetical Pastoral Institute, but my educational experiences were eclipsed by the news that my friend Father Ben was going to leave in July for Japan to teach at Sophia University. If all went well, he would transfer to the Jesuit Province in Japan. I did not realize how I had counted on his strong presence in my life. In July, another Sister and I took him to the airport.

☙

I still had my Sister friends. But because I did not like myself, I depended on outside affirmation and a strong element of that was gone. Of course my drinking increased. I believed that if anyone knew of my weakness as I regarded it, respect for me would be lost. It was a very lonely time.

Sister Maryanne, a younger, gentle Sister, was our Abbess at that time. In the summer of 1970, she had spent three months at the International Yoga Institute in New York State. During Lent she led yoga meditations with women religious in New Orleans. The first year she offered them, I was recovering from bone surgery and could not physically participate, but I sat in the room enjoying the quiet and the peace.

In my turmoil I yearned to possess her tranquility. In 1973, Sister Maryanne made a retreat at Father William McNamara's center in the desert near Sedona, Arizona. Encouraged by her example, I asked permission to spend two weeks there in May 1974. The retreat center was in an area of magnificent rock formations and wide-open spaces. Only the occasional howl of coyote during the night broke the silence. There was a large main building containing the underground chapel, a large dining area, kitchen, and other spaces.

Each of us at the retreat had our own hermitage. Mine was very small—just one room with a small bathroom, a table and chair, a hot plate, and a narrow bed. Perishables could be kept in a refrigerator in the main building. To help with my expenses, I weeded the cactus gardens and arranged correspondence between Nada and a new center, Nova Nada, in Nova Scotia. When I asked if I could read the correspondence, they freely gave permission. I found the back-and-forth of letters about starting a new enterprise very interesting.

I arose each day before dawn, read my breviary, and watched the sun rise behind the red rocks. Then I ate breakfast and ran along the nearby unpaved roads. After that, I weeded or worked on the correspondence. Except for one lunch,

I ate my meals in my small hermitage. Looking back after so many years, I am amazed that I had no alcohol with me. It was a peace-filled time with days of quiet and natural beauty. At the end of these two weeks, a former Poor Clare and her friend picked me up and took me to Phoenix for a Mexican supper. We drove up a mountain overlooking the city where we had a spectacular view of city lights. The next morning one of the women took me to the airport to return home to New Orleans. My drinking resumed.

Shortly after, word came that Ben would be returning to Loyola to resume teaching. I felt grateful for his return but sorry that things had not worked out as he had hoped.

During that summer, an elderly Jesuit professor at Loyola offered a course in Greek poetry which I signed up for––the only person who did! When he discovered I had studied Greek, he insisted on using the Greek version. He was in his element. Together we drank many cups of extremely sweet chicory coffee and I struggled with the Greek. Teaching was his life. He wanted to continue our daily hour together until Loyola reopened, but I knew it was time to end the study sessions after six weeks, as planned.

At the monastery I liked taking my turn as cook and preparing food for a couple of medical diets. I also prepared liturgies during the week and enjoyed my Sister friends both in the monastery and outside. But alcohol continued to be a secret and guilty part of my life.

Ben returned later in the summer in time to resume teaching history at Loyola and to institute a class in Zen meditation. He enriched students' experience by including Ikebana flower arranging, which he had been doing for years, but now had became a Master. He also studied and wrote haiku. I enrolled in the meditation class along with my doctor's wife, plus a vibrant young wife and mother, and a wealthy older woman, a real character whom we named the "Delta Queen." A Sister in Pastoral Ministry at Loyola who had become a good friend joined us. She had a warm personality and a delicious sense of humor. Because of an amusing story she told about an incident in her Bostonian childhood, we called her "Blessed Imelda." The class proved to be extremely popular and was extended through the year.

Each day I arrived at Loyola attired in contemporary dress, which was a brown skirt, white blouse and a veil that I removed in the locker room. I donned a pair of slacks kept for the occasion in a friend's locker. One day as I walked out dressed for a class, a student asked, "Weren't you a nun when you went in there?"

In the spring, a married couple offered Ben their large home near Lake Pontchartrain for a weekend Zen retreat. For once I had no wine in my suitcase. We older women were given a large bedroom while the younger students slept in sleeping bags in a main room. The first evening four of us decided we didn't want to be separate so we took our sleeping bags and joined them (to their and Ben's delight). For me the retreat was an oasis of peace—long periods of Zazen, quiet instructions from Ben, preparing and sharing meals.

଼

As a community experiment, we were each given $5.00 a month for personal use, a practice unheard of among the Poor Clares. Mine was spent on wine and perhaps a small treat for Elizabeth, my closest friend in the community. Also I "borrowed" money from petty cash. I was truly deluded enough to believe that the next month I would reimburse it out of my $5.00. Several years later, when I was in treatment, Sister Francis Clare told my counselor I had taken money from the community. I was genuinely horrified. So persuaded was I that I would pay it back, I denied ever having stolen money to buy wine

Early on after my arrival in New Orleans, I learned how to take buses to a Winn Dixie grocery store or to K & B drug stores where one could buy wine. I also purchased pretty paper napkins so the clerks would assume it was for a party. When we had a party, I provided wine for the Sisters. When I made a large pot of red beans and rice for the occupants of Assisi Hall where we lived at St. Teresa's, I added wine to it—all legitimate reasons for buying wine, in my judgment.

By 1975, I had nearly enough credits to graduate from college. To my wonder, now as I look back on my increasing use of alcohol, I had an excellent academic record at both St. Teresa's and at Loyola, as well as in other classes I had taken in New Orleans at Xavier and the Catechetical and Pastoral Institute. Father Hervig Artz, a Belgian Jesuit and author who was a close friend of Sister Helen Rolfson, was scheduled to teach a class on Western mystics that summer. Following that, he was also scheduled to give a retreat.

Our Abbess, Sister Francis Clare, gave me permission to return to St. Teresa's and obtain my degree. My drinking had progressed to a point where in spite of being close to a beloved friend and enjoying the class (and later, the retreat), I kept drinking secretly. I even took some of the beer Helen kept in the refrigerator for Father Artz. Feelings of guilt continued to follow me. Shortly before I left for home, I bought some special chocolates to take to our community. I stored them in the refrigerator. Someone opened them and removed several from the box. When I shared this with Helen, she sympathized with me and told me someone had also taken some of the beer she had bought for Father Artz. Even as I spent eight weeks happily studying and enjoying the visits with Helen, the beautiful campus, and biking to downtown Winona, shame and guilt were my constant companions.

☙

After my return to the monastery, life continued as usual. After so many years, I cannot remember many particulars. There were problems in the monastery. Due to my alcoholism I could not adequately deal with them and support the faithful women who bore the burden.

Our leadership changed in the spring of 1976. The Sister who had been elected Abbess decided we should bring in outside help to restore our peace and the healthy living of our life of prayer. As time went on, another Sister and I, discouraged with the direction our meetings were taking, decided to take a leave of absence for six months. (She returned before six months had passed. I did not and received an extension.)

Because two of us took a leave, the community could only afford to provide each of us one half of the usual amount of support given to Sisters on leave. Fortunately, one of the two women who had been part of our community from 1970-1972, had urged me, if ever I decided to ask for a leave of absence, to spend a month with her in her small convent in a beautiful part of New York State. On a trip lasting a few days, I took a bus from New Orleans to Canandaigua, New York, to join her and her Sisters for four weeks. Looking back I believe that was the time I bought a bottle of wine and sat in the back of the bus with an open bottle. I could have been arrested during that trip. Somehow, no one noticed it!

My hope was that as part of my leave I could make a 30-day directed retreat at a Jesuit retreat center in Guelph, Ontario. Ben knew my desire to do that. To my astonishment, he obtained a loan for it from his Jesuit superior at Loyola. There was no repayment date. At the end of the retreat, I was given an envelop with instructions not to open it until after my return to New Orleans. It contained the money for the retreat.

In early November, I took a bus from New York to Guelph, arriving a day early. I have two amusing memories of that day. I had been assigned to a room at the retreat that had formerly been occupied by a priest. He had been moved to another part of the building. Most of that first day, I spent in catching up on correspondence with family and friends. That evening I retired early. At about eleven o'clock, I was suddenly awakened by the overhead light to find an elderly priest gazing down at me. Somehow he had not received word of the room change!

The other memory involved the secretary who rang my doorbell the next morning. In embarrassment, she handed me some Canadian stamps saying, "Sister, you used American postage on all of your mail yesterday. I put Canadian postage on it for you and brought you some extra postage." It had not occurred to me that I was in another country.

I had a fine retreat master, a young and perceptive Jesuit who almost immediately recognized my self-hatred and commented on it. But he did not suspect that alcoholism played a large part in it. I had a difficult time with the Ignatian way of prayer and the use of my imagination. Although I longed just to BE and not try to put myself into Biblical scenes, I applied myself to it as he asked. I believe I benefited from it. Most of all, I had a measure of peace because I was not drinking. I have always been grateful for the experience.

☙

The retreat ended around the first of December. I initially expected to return to New Orleans. Sister Fara had invited me to stay with her and her Eucharistic Missionaries of St. Dominic in their large convent on Magazine Street. The first floor was a center for the surrounding community. The Sisters lived upstairs. However, because Sisters would be returning from their missions over the Christmas season, there would be no room for me until after the New Year. My Sister of St. Joseph friend arranged for me to stay until January with a couple who were friends of hers in Buffalo, New York.

The wife and mother was blind. It was remarkable what she could do. The couple's older son was in the seminary, one daughter was married, and their sixteen-year-old son and fourteen-year-old daughter were at home. They also had a dog and a cat. I slept in a twin bed in the fourteen-year-old's room. The first night she asked me to choose between having the cat or the dog sleep with me. I chose the cat as the smaller of the two animals. The next morning I was awakened early by the cat on my head. The family was very good to me, but I felt out of place. I began to take long walks as I had in Canandaigua to find places where I could buy wine.

At Christmas, the elder son returned home with a very bad cold and the flu from the minor seminary. His father thought some brandy might be helpful, but I remember recommending port wine. When a winter storm enveloped Buffalo and made getting out impossible for me, I helped myself to a "little" port wine. Before I realized it, the bottle was nearly empty and I refilled it with water. That evening, the young seminarian came to supper looking miserable and ill. His father asked, "Isn't the port wine helping at all?" I wanted to disappear under the rug when he replied, "Dad, that port wine tastes just like water!" Recollections of that month remain hazy but tinged with a bleak feeling of sadness.

In January, I was on my way back to New Orleans to stay with Fara at the Eucharistic Missionaries. At that time, I desired to obtain a Master's degree in Spirituality. In spite of my alcoholism, my marks were excellent at every place I had studied. But the program was new and no scholarships were available. The Benedictine Sister who had been working with our community advised me to take Clinical Pastoral Education (CPE) at Southern Baptist Hospital as that institution offered a stipend to seminarians and to Sisters. Although I had no desire to be a chaplain, I applied and was accepted. I cannot remember when the program opened in the winter of 1977, but I took the bus and attended everyday.

Meanwhile, my drinking continued. In the convent, it became harder to hide. One night, a collision happened on the street outside of my bedroom window. The Coordinator and her assistant knocked on my door and asked to come in and look out of the window. I knew I smelled of alcohol and tried to be calm and cool. The next day they confronted me about my drinking—the first time since one Sister in the Poor Clares had done so in the monastery in Minnesota. I was extremely embarrassed and knew I had to move. I no longer have much recollection of how long I had been there nor how events proceeded. At one point a Sister who taught at Loyola invited me to move into a back room of her elderly mother's home near the monastery. I lived there while I attended CPE.

More than six months passed since I took my leave because basically nothing had changed in my personal life. I was going nowhere in spite of enjoying good relationships with the others in my CPE group. I don't remember drinking before I attended CPE sessions in the afternoon nor before my overnights at the hospital, but alcohol was a daily companion.

In the spring, the Baptist minister in charge of the program invited us all to his country home for an afternoon of friendly companionship and food. Two events stand out in my mind. A five-year-old boy taught me how to open oysters and eat them raw, and another member of our small group flew his ancient two-seater plane to the gathering and took me for a flight. It was wonderful! Together we sat in the small plane with an expanse of glass in front of us and surveyed the earth below.

Knowing that I did not plan to become a hospital chaplain, I left CPE and was hired as an admitting clerk at Southern Baptist Hospital. It was my first experience with computers and I found it fascinating. However, my alcoholism was progressing. To make it acceptable, I had wine in a lovely glass each day at lunch—sometimes, more than one. One incident stands out as a low moment that filled me with shame. A black woman took my place at the admitting station so I could have a few minutes off. When another white clerk came in and told me in horror that she could smell alcohol on the other woman's breath, I knew the smell of alcohol had come from me and not the black clerk. But I kept silent.

Reflections of that time continue to be vague. I suppose I took a bus back to where I was staying when I left the hospital at night. I cannot remember how I met a taxi driver who insisted on picking me up and driving me home each night, as he was concerned about my safety. We must have had a connection. It seems strange to me now. He never let me pay.

☙

In the summer of 1977, I was asked to be part of a meeting called "Monks East and West" in Massachusetts. I was delighted. The meeting of Benedictine and Trappist Catholic Monks and Sisters with Monks of other Eastern religions, mostly Buddhists, was held at a Trappist monastery. Monks came from Europe and the East, from India and Thailand. Swami Satchidananda, whom I had met a few years earlier in New Orleans, was there. He left me with a memory I'll never forget. Each day we had daily Mass while sitting on the floor. No one was forbidden to receive Communion. As I sat down, after having received the host one morning, I happened to look up as Swami returned to his place. His face was transfigured with awe and joy. I had to look down. I thought, he doesn't believe as I do, but he is experiencing the Holy. I was deeply moved. I'd like to say that I did not drink during those days, but that's not true. One day I slipped into the room where Mass was offered and drank some Mass wine. In many ways it was a time of joy for me, but as usual, it was clouded with guilt.

☙

After my return to New Orleans, I moved into a home with an elderly Catholic widow. Why or how I changed my living place I can't recall. I had to find a job as I had left my job in the admitting office at Southern Baptist Hospital. Several friends were keeping eyes and ears open about work I might find to support myself. More than once the morning after a call the previous evening, I was unable to read the information I had written down. Shame kept me from calling the friends and asking them to repeat the message. However, the daily paper carried the news that D.H. Holmes, an upscale department store on Canal Street, would soon open a store quite near to where I was living. I called for information and discovered there was an opening for someone to work in the book department on Canal Street. I applied and was immediately hired.

My fantasy of having time to read soon met the reality of a book department kept busy by tourists looking for reading matter for their travels. Mostly they were interested in Louis L'Amour for the men and new novels for the women. The other employees welcomed me. Since I was not paying for lodging, I was able to save some money even though the pay was low and my drinking continued in the evenings. I attended early Mass with the woman with whom I lived and returned home afterwards for breakfast before I left for work.

Each day I ate a quick lunch in the rather small windowless room reserved for department meetings and then roamed the French Quarter. One day when I was alone in the book department, the friendly young man who headed the department next to ours stopped by and said, "Miz Catherine, may I ask you a question?"

Surprised, I answered, "Of course, Joe."

He asked, "Were you a school teacher?"

"No, Joe," I answered.

He looked disappointed and said, "I can almost always tell what profession a person is in. Every time I see you, I say 'She's either a nun or a school teacher and she wouldn't be working here if she were a nun.'"

"You're right on one count, Joe," I answered. "I am a nun."

He was delighted. Every time he passed through the book department after that, he waved and called out, "Hi, Sister!" Customers looked around in bewilderment.

Things went well at D.H. Holmes. I had friends and I liked my co-workers, but I missed religious life. The Sisters at the Bloomington monastery had been sending me an amount of money each month. I longed to return there but did not view that as a possibility nor did I feel ready to return to the Poor Clares in New Orleans. I still did not realize the part alcoholism was playing in my life. Shame kept me silent and deluded. So I wrote a letter to the Provincial of the Sisters of St. Joseph in the St. Paul Province. She invited me for an interview. Thus, in the fall of 1977, I flew to St. Paul. I thought our visit went quite well, but no decisions were made except to continue communicating.

At around this time, through Sister Fara, I had met an elderly woman in New Orleans, another true character. She identified herself as Anglican and belonged to the Anglican Cathedral in New Orleans. Religion played a central place in her life. She read serious religious literature but had no radio or television. She faced herself honestly and everyone else the same way--imperious and caustic in her wit. She belonged to an old aristocratic but impoverished Louisiana family. Due to two failed marriages and a tragedy in her life, she led a rather lonely life. For some reason she liked me. Although we had some deep disagreements, especially regarding racial issues (she regarded blacks as inferior in intelligence to whites), I eventually realized I could not change her attitudes. She was deeply honest and outspoken and there was a goodness and kindness in her I liked.

During my leave of absence, she quite frequently invited me for meals, simple and elegantly prepared. I cannot remember ever having wine or other alcoholic beverages at her home. Later, to my dismay, my Abbess blamed her for my alcoholism. When my elderly friend learned of my being in treatment, she was shocked but our friendship continued. In later years, she twice paid my airfare so I could fly to Baton Rouge and visit her in the retirement home where she died several years later.

After Christmas in 1977, I returned to St. Paul for another visit with the Provincial, Sister Kathleen Marie. Strangely, I have no recollection of how it went, but an event happened on the second day of my stay that devastated and haunted me for a long time. I had spent the night with my brother and sister-in-law. After they left for Saturday morning errands, I took the bag of alcohol bottles I needed to dispose of and headed down the road to a wooded area near their home. Houses were far apart. I looked for a secluded place to toss the bag. Suddenly, I heard a loud voice shouting, "Get out of here, walking weirdo! Get out of here!" I looked off to the right and saw a man standing outside his home. "Yes, I mean you walking weirdo! Get out of here!" I turned and fled. Was this what I had become?

That evening or the next evening, I returned to New Orleans. As the plane was nearly empty, we few passengers were invited to come up to first class and were served drinks. I accepted hard liquor, which I wasn't used to. By the time the plane reached New Orleans, I was drunk and slurring my speech. Ben picked me up at around midnight, New Year's Day to take me home. I'm sure I was babbling. He turned the car radio up. He was upset. I continued the ride in silence and shame. When we reached the house, I had trouble getting the key into the lock but finally succeeded and went in. It was the day after New Year's, 1978.

The next morning as Mrs. L. and I ate breakfast, the doorbell rang. It was the mail carrier who handed me my key. I'd left it outside. Mrs. L. was horrified and angry. Anyone could have entered the house during the night. One did not leave a front door unlocked at night in New Orleans, especially not with a key in the lock.

One afternoon shortly after my return, I went to see the Sister who had been helping our community. At lunch, I had been drinking. I had not used mouthwash afterwards. As I walked in, she exclaimed, "Of course! It's alcohol. I knew there was something, but I could never identify what was wrong. I think it's wonderful that you may be going to Minnesota. They have Hazelden and the Johnston Institute. They can help you there! May I call Sister Kathleen Marie and share this with her?"

Stunned, I said, "Yes."

☙

After my return home, I felt hopeless and dismayed. My thoughts were raging! "I am not a sick person! I won't go up there as a sick person!" That evening I received a call from Sister Kathleen Marie. I knew I was slurring my speech as I tried to explain that I had my partials out. I informed her that I had decided to return to the New Orleans Monastery. She sounded relieved and agreed that was the best thing to do. A few days later I made arrangements to return to the monastery in August after I had attended St. Bonaventure's University in Oleans, New York. It amazes me, as I write this, that I had been able to save enough money for summer school. I am sure that the fact that I was not paying rent enabled me to do so.

I continued working at the D.H. Holmes department store until the summer. When I left, my co-workers and the women in giftwrap gave me a large, beautifully illustrated book about gnomes that was extremely popular at that time. I felt quite overwhelmed by their kindness. Soon I left New Orleans by Greyhound Bus. I rode to St. Paul to spend a few days with my brothers and then to my uncle's and aunt's farm in southern Minnesota where I had spent happy childhood days. Next I went to Winona to spend a short time with Sister Helen before I continued on to New York and St. Bonaventure's.

The six weeks in that beautiful area of New York were busy and fairly peaceful. I enjoyed my classes and the companionship of Sisters from that area and various parts of the United States and Ireland. Where I bought wine during those six weeks, I cannot remember, but I know I did. I could not go through a day without it.

On the Feast of St. Bonaventure, a few young seminarians took some of us to Niagara Falls. I think we took a picnic lunch. In the afternoon I craved alcohol. Unable to find a place that sold it, I went into a nice restaurant and nearly begged to buy a bottle of wine. As the time passed and it became time to return to my monastery, I became more depressed. I had been out of the monastery for nearly two years and had not resolved anything. Of course my active alcoholism as a cause never entered my mind.

Two young Franciscan Sisters were driving home to Louisiana and they asked me to join them, which I gratefully did. The ride was more enjoyable than another long bus ride. It provided me with Sister companionship as I prepared to reenter the monastery.

☙

My depression increased along with my drinking. I kept "borrowing" from petty cash to buy wine. As time went on, I found it harder and harder to hide. Neither prayer nor will power seemed to help. I never tried to quit--I tried to control.

Sometimes Sisters from other communities came to our monastery for quiet retreats. Sometimes in the evening, one would ask to see me. Feeling unworthy because I thought I was a "bad nun," I had a glass of wine to fortify myself, followed by mouthwash.

During our annual fall bazaar, I spent two days making bread, which was very popular. That year I also took orders for fruitcakes. I was quite overwhelmed by the numbers of orders (which of course required alcohol). As we had no guests in our extern apartment, I did my baking there which provided me with privacy. For the first time, I bought brandy, which I began to consume. The fruitcakes were made free of alcohol.

I decided the cakes would be fine if I could get more alcohol to just pour over them before wrapping them up. I still had a few weeks so I called a liquor store with an Italian name as I thought the owner was surely Catholic. I told him about my fruitcake baking to aid the monastery. I fully intended to abide by my plan. He personally arrived with a half gallon bottle of brandy. A few weeks later the fruitcakes were picked up without a drop of alcohol in or on them.

One evening as I worked on the baking in a haze, a Franciscan priest who was visiting our monastery was seemingly casually walking past the kitchen door several times. I believe he reported to Mother Francis Clare what he observed. I think it was quite obvious. However, I somehow produced fruitcakes.

CB

After many years I cannot be sure of chronology of events during these last months of my drinking, but I know I was getting more and more unable to hide it. I was living against my own principles, and I was miserable.

The following incidents are out of order but remain vivid in my mind. On one trip from St. Teresa's in Winona, Minnesota, to New Orleans, three of us from our monastery sat in the Minneapolis - St. Paul airport waiting to board our plane. Before we left Winona, I had been unable to dispose of my bottles, so I wrapped them in a brown paper bag and carried them in a large, colorful plastic bag. On top of them I had placed several light packages. Suddenly, I announced I needed to use the restroom and picked up my bag. One of the Sisters said, "Don't take that heavy bag. We'll watch it." I made some remark about needing it and went off to leave the bag of bottles in a stall. One day several months later, this Sister asked, "Katie, do you remember our sitting in the airport and you went off to the ladies room with your heavy bag? When you came back, it was light. What did you have in that bag, Katie?" I can't remember my answer.

On New Year's Eve, a bottle of wine and crackers or cookies were left out for a short celebration of the New Year after Midnight Mass. As no one was around, I imbibed quite freely of the wine and went to take a short nap before Mass. I don't remember if anyone tried to wake me before Mass, but if so, she did not succeed. I missed the Mass.

The new year dawned, a lovely, cool, sunny morning as I walked through Audubon Park to Mass at Loyola. I remember rejoicing that it was a fresh new year, full of promise of change. I felt grateful for a fresh start. Life was going to be different! I don't remember anyone having said anything to me about my absence from Mass. Perhaps someone did.

In February, two or three of us went with our Abbess for a weekend to a midlife workshop given by a well-known Franciscan Father. One of the presentations was about alcoholism. Had she spoken to him about my drinking? Was this talk the reason she wanted me to attend? I felt very uncomfortable.

It may have been in that spring of 1979 that I also shared my alcohol problem with a trusted Jesuit. He did not believe I was truly an alcoholic. I'm sure I minimized my intake, but at some point I also decided I had to go to Confession. Of course I did not go to the priest who came to the monastery because I was sure he would recognize my voice, so I went to a parish church one afternoon. With fear I told the Priest I drank "too much."

It was a disaster. He quite literally shouted at me, "You're a nun?"

"Yes, Father."

"And you drink?"

"Yes, Father."

"I never thought a nun would drink! Sister, I'll tell you what to do. Every afternoon drink a quart of orange juice and I guarantee you won't drink anything more that evening."

As I have said when I have shared my story, I never tried that so I don't know if that works or not. In shame I left the church.

Two other significant events from that period also come to mind as I write. Our community belonged to the Association of Contemplative Nuns, women from all over the country. At their January meeting I was asked to edit their newsletter. With trepidation, I agreed. Memories of it are vague. I can no longer remember how often it was to come out, but I do know I did not succeed in editing an edition until the following August. My friend, Virgie, who had often invited me for supper when I was on leave of absence, took me to the printers. When we picked up copies, in gratitude, I gave her one. That evening, forthright as always, she called me and told me I should be ashamed of all the obvious mistakes in it. I did not do another one.

That spring I sought out a well-known Dominican Sister to be my Spiritual Director. Again, I shared my concern about alcohol, but not completely truthfully. Like my Jesuit confessor and friend, she did not think I was an alcoholic. She suggested I take a protein snack with me when I devoted time to prayer in late afternoon, a vulnerable time of day. She advised me to dialogue with "Brother Port" (one of my favorite drinks). As I read the dialogue now, I find it quite delusional. It makes a plan to drink with reverence for one of God's gifts and not abuse alcohol, which is impossibility for an alcoholic. But my director didn't think I was one.

At around that time, a couple of the Sisters had gone to the Abbess about my drinking. She confronted me one day. I agreed that I was indeed drinking too much and promised to drink only when we had wine for a special celebration. Of course I could not do that. One day shortly after that, I took a cold beer from the refrigerator to my room and drank it. A few minutes later I met her in the hallway and she said, "You've been drinking." I denied it, and she remarked, "That's the first time you've ever lied to me." I felt angry with myself and ashamed, but I could not own the truth and apologize to her.

In April, I attended an Intensive Journal Workshop, again seeking Marianne's peace as she had attended one the previous spring. Journaling became part of my prayers for several months. Entry after entry expresses my intense desire for alcohol and my disgust with what I considered my weakness. It is difficult to read them now:

"I wish my life did not revolve around drink—the longing for sherry or port—the depression because I drank, especially since I had promised not to."

"Where am I now in my life? Trying to come to grips with the meaning of my life—faithful to my call from Our Lord—trying to escape from feeling a failure through alcohol; this had been reported to the Provincial—embarrassing to me—frightening."

"Since it makes me so miserable, why do I do it?"

"I am really depressed and afraid F. will go into my room and find the bottle in my wastebasket… I hope I shall be given another chance and not be found out—I feel apprehensive. In order to be free, I have to be true." (This was written at the workshop.)

"I long to be true, but the effort to live without wine seems so very difficult. I haven't found any other way of relaxing or escaping from pressure, loneliness or boredom that seems so good. I know prayer should enable me to deal with life fully and positively—but I find the effort too much even though I want it."

"I spend so much energy on getting wine—and then I can't stand myself. I have an inner need to be true. It's like living a lie—and not fulfilling…. I wonder if I can become whole and well again… I feel much shame about the me I have come to know."

"I ask God again and again for help, but here I still am—crying out from my near despair, my depression. I rarely feel lighthearted as I used to—I rarely want to face a new day."

"I don't feel comfortable with myself. Other people seem stronger than I. I feel shame and anger at them for exposing me. I feel anger with myself for having proved so weak. I'd like to go back and make a fresh start."

"F. asked me to go to the convenience store and get soft drinks and tomatoes for supper tonight. I got money enough from the portress room and the gift shop so I could buy wine. I think M. saw me with the gift shop box open. On the way to the store, I decided not to buy wine, so I have to return the money. I wonder if I would return it had she not seen the open drawer?"

Several years ago, I highlighted the preceding passages from my Intensive Journals in a presentation at an Alcoholic Anonymous meeting on Step 1, which is "(We) admitted we were powerless over alcohol—that our lives had become unmanageable." My journal is filled with recriminations because of buying and drinking alcohol. Remorse followed because I had promised not to drink. Knowing I was being watched, I was afraid of being found out. I felt like a failure as a woman religious. I felt anger towards God who I believed was not answering my prayers. I never wanted to quit. I wanted to control my drinking. I could not imagine life without alcohol. Yet at times I wrote thoughtful and prayerful reflections and even had an article about contemplative prayer published.

One of the Sisters who made retreats at the monastery asked me to be her Director. I felt like a phony.

※

For a couple of weeks during the summer of 1979, I was confined to the infirmary with a large hematoma in my leg. It was a time of comparative peace, quiet, and reading. During that time I wrote the following in my journal, "We contemplative religious should take the time to be open and to listen to God so that when He comes, we can experience His Presence and spread the good news that He IS, He COMES, and He CARES for each of us human beings. Surely that is our apostolate. Many today do not take the time to wait upon the Lord and receive Him when He comes. But our lifestyle provides for that. We must be a sign of hope and love for alienated men and women of our time. I guess I can say, 'Blessed be the hematoma in my leg!'"

During these months and years, I also had several hospital stays for a foot infection, bone surgeries and precancerous growths removed. I actually peacefully welcomed them because I knew I could not obtain alcohol.

Most of the Sisters in the community were not aware or were denying the "elephant in the room," but I knew the abbess and one or two others were watching me. One afternoon when I was portress, I arranged to have a friend bring me a bottle of wine ("for cooking," of course). When it arrived I put it in the wastebasket and covered it with papers while I went off to supper. When I returned to the office, it was gone. I decided to react angrily, broadcasting that I had put a bottle of wine in the wastebasket, which I had been given for a special recipe, until my return, and someone had taken it! The announcement was greeted with silence.

As summer drew to an end, I prepared to leave for a month-long celebration at the Bloomington monastery. Twenty-five years before, in 1954, we had formally opened the monastery. Now it was their Silver Jubilee, and they invited me to share it with them. Sister Francis Clare had given me permission to go. I was determined to show her that I would not need to abuse alcohol while I was there. My brother picked me up at the airport. On the way to the monastery, I prevailed upon him to stop and buy a bottle of wine as a gift for the Sisters.

☙

Prior to that time, I had taken an evening class in Russian literature at Loyola University; and for a class project at the end, I had painted a picture of Mary, which resembled a Russian icon. The professor, a Russian woman, liked it and showed it to an Orthodox Bishop who came to New Orleans to found a congregation there. He came to see me one day and asked me to do an icon for his church. He was extremely poor. I was certainly open to the idea, so I arranged with one of the Sisters in the Bloomington monastery who was an iconographer to teach me how to paint one properly during my month there.

In preparation, I drew an outline of Our Mother of Tenderness to take with me and transfer to a prepared wooden background. Then I would paint it while also learning how to prepare another large background for an icon. In this way, I could learn the many steps necessary to paint a true icon. I fully expected to return to our New Orleans monastery and become an iconographer as a way of engaging in a work I loved and in helping to support the monastery.

After Mass and breakfast every morning, Sister J. and I sat side by side while she painted an icon of the Baptism of our Lord. She also instructed me, step by step, on how to mix the egg and the natural earth powders to obtain the colors needed. Day by day, an icon emerged.

In the afternoons, I took the money Sister Francis Clare had given me before I left and went out walking to find a liquor store—something I had not needed to do in New Orleans.

October gave way to November, cold, rainy and snowy. One afternoon I had nothing to drink, and I craved alcohol, so I asked one of the Sisters for a key, as I needed to get out and walk. She said, "Katie, it's cold and raining. If you need to walk, you can walk out in the yard." (They had four enclosed acres.)

I insisted, "No, I have to get out." In tears, she handed me the keys.

One day the Sister who was preparing a special prayer for that evening asked me to read a beautiful prayer. That morning I was determined not to drink that day and to read well. By evening I was drunk. I could barely see as we had only candlelight, and I could hear myself slurring the words. I felt mortified. The following morning I apologized to her, and she replied, "You were 'three sheets to the wind.'"

During that time I tried to con myself into believing I was at peace over the decision I had made in April 1959 to return to the Sauk Rapids monastery and later to transfer to the monastery in New Orleans. I even wrote a poem expressing my inner peace. My inner pain and depression belied that fanciful thinking. The icon was nearly finished except for a few minor details when I left the monastery to return to New Orleans on November 19. Again, my brother, Bob, picked me up to take me to the airport. As we drove away, I looked back to see all of the Sisters at the Bloomington monastery standing outside waving, "Goodbye."

I felt like a character in a comic strip at that time, "Li'l Abner." He was a little man in a black bowler hat with a black cloud over his head. I knew that something was going to happen, and I thought to myself, "I am flying into my doom."

The next day I walked over to the 7-11 store near the monastery and bought a bottle of wine. It was a gray, overcast day. My feet felt like two blocks of lead. I kept repeating to myself, "I am walking into my doom." But I went. In the evening we had a festive dinner to celebrate the birthday of a ninety-year-old member of the community, followed by a special movie. I fell asleep with a cup of wine beside my chair.

℃ℨ

The following afternoon, I was called to the Abbess' office and told to close the door and sit down. The moment I had dreaded had arrived. It was initiated, as I later learned, by a call from the Abbess of the Bloomington Monastery urging Sister Francis Clare to get help for me and suggesting she call Hazelden. Hazelden staff suggested the treatment center in Baton Rouge. Sister Francis Clare informed me that my suitcase was in my room and I was to pack it. Of course I begged her to give me "one more month," but she had done her homework by seeking information from a Franciscan priest. She replied in a loud and decisive voice, "You can't quit! You're an alcoholic!"

On the way to my room, I tried to make three phone calls, not to be rescued but to inform them where I was going. I did not reach either my spiritual director or Ben. Only Fara was at home. She sounded shocked. I assume one of the few Sisters who knew what was going on reported to Sister Francis Clare who came immediately and ordered me not to leave my room. I'm sure they thought I was trying to be "rescued." I wasn't. I knew it was inevitable. At about 4:00 P.M., we set out for Baton Rouge, one of the younger Sisters driving. I had a lump in my throat and I could not speak.

When we arrived at Baton Rouge General Hospital, we headed for the admitting office where I had to fill out a page of information. In reply to "reason for admission," I looked at Sister Francis Clare who said, "Alcoholism!" I silently wrote that down and was immensely relieved when the admitting clerk said, "You won't be staying here. The treatment center is a few blocks down the street." Both of my companions were wearing their veils. I did not want anyone to know I was a nun.

Supper was ending as we entered the Chemical Dependency Unit in Baton Rouge. To my dismay, a kindly older nurse insisted we have supper before the two Sisters left. I wanted them to leave immediately. A young woman who was nearing the end of her stay was asked to sit with us. Sister Francis Clare asked her many questions. I could not eat a bite. Finally, after what seemed to me an eternity, the Sisters left. On returning from the door, I met a smiling woman in the hall. She held out her hand saying, "Hi, I'm A. I'm an alcoholic." I replied, "Hi, I'm Catherine, I don't know if I'm an alcoholic." She laughed and said, "Oh, you don't know, huh?" Later that evening I felt a strange peace and thought, "I'm with my people."

The following day, Thanksgiving, there was a small staff. I was asked to sit with a woman who was coming off Valium and alert the nurse if she began to seizure. At times the whole bed shook. It was a somber experience.

On Saturday all fifty-two of us gathered with a counselor in a large gymnasium-like room. As we went around the room and introduced ourselves, I said, "Hi I'm Catherine. I'm an alcoholic. I drank sherry."

Bill from Chattanooga, Tennessee, called out, "We don't care what you drank, Catherine. You're just an alcoholic like the rest of us!" Everyone laughed. As the days went by, he and I became friends.

Patients came from all over the southern region of our country. With the probable exception of the adolescents, we were in mixed-aged groups. I was ready for help. I didn't experience the deep shame I often felt around non-alcoholic visitors whom patients at Baton Rouge jokingly called "earth people." The shame for being an alcoholic continued for some time in recovery. I wrote to family and close friends and apologized for being an alcoholic. It took time and education to eradicate that. Most of us were serious about recovery and we felt sorry for those who were not.

Two of us were severely hypoglycemic and were on a strict diet. Everyone else was on a low sugar and low carb diet. No candy was allowed. Each morning we exercised, had group (I think twice a day) with our counselor. We watched appropriate movies and /or heard AA speakers who came in for meetings in the evenings. The program was 12-step based. We formed bonds with other patients. For years afterwards, I kept up a correspondence with my first roommate from Birmingham, Alabama.

I became friendly with another patient, a man of about my age, who I felt was lonely. He was designing a house, which he later hoped to build. He shared the details and drawings with me. I had no romantic interest in him so I was amused when several of the women came to me one day, deeply concerned that he was "hitting" on me. Because I was a nun, they thought I should be warned!

Another incident impressed me. An attractive young member of our group had run away from home in Baton Rouge and had gone to California where she got into the wrong crowd and was gang raped. She seemed serious about sobriety and agreed to go to a halfway house for an extended stay before she returned home to be with her family. Our counselor announced in group that she would be leaving. She gave him permission to share with us what she'd suggested when he told her that she abstain from sex for at least six months after she left the halfway house as part of her recovery plan. She told him she thought she should abstain for at least a year. He then asked if any one of us would agree to do that. When I raised my hand, everyone burst into laughter. The counselor said, "I forgot about you!"

The third Saturday in treatment a young man and I were chosen to go shopping at the nearby drugstore for items the patients needed. They had turned their requests into the office. We were given money to pay for items needed. Several patients secretly asked us to bring them a candy bar or two. I was sure that the staff knew this occurred but chose to focus on more important issues. I don't remember if we bought candy or not. But I remember it in connection with what happened during Family Week.

Time drew near for Family Week––a week to which we invited the people who had been most affected by our using drugs or drinking. We were allowed to sit in and observe other patients' family week. We had to choose whom we wanted there. No one could choose for us. My two brothers in Minnesota chose not to come, but the four Sisters I asked all came: Sisters Francis Clare; Elizabeth, my closest friend in our community; Charlene, whose Novice Mistress I had been; and Anne Condon, the founder of the Bloomington monastery whom I had walked out on in 1959.

I thought the Sisters might be uncomfortable, but they arrived early each morning and sat in the meeting room. Elizabeth's birthday occurred during the week. I got a card for her. The previous evening I had visited the woman with whom I had initially roomed and told her and her roommate I wished I had gift for her—at least a chocolate bar that she liked. They laughed and told me to look under the pads in the Kotex box. I found a layer of Hershey bars. The next morning I went into the meeting room early and gave Elizabeth her card in which I had put the bar. Laughing, I said, "There's contraband material in there!"

Later, when our meeting was scheduled, I walked into the room to find the counselor looking stern and the Sisters upset. Elizabeth was crying. She said, "Katie, I thought you were serious about treatment. I can't eat that candy bar." Francis Clare, clearly angry, said, "I thought this was an honesty program." And the counselor demanded to know where I had gotten the candy bar. From there it escalated. There was no way I was going to get my two new friends in trouble. It seemed to go on and on. Eventually I broke down and cried hysterically. (The only time that had happened previously was when my dad took my mother to the TB ward. I was fourteen then, forty-two years before this incident. I thought I should never see my mother alive again. It took my aunt and my dad to separate us.)

As we left the room, a young male patient walked me down to where my two roommates were waiting for me. He told them to take care of me because I was in a "bad way." The rest is a blur until my group counselor told me I could have a pass to return home with the Sisters that afternoon and return to the chemical dependency unit on Sunday evening. I was surprised and responded, "I thought I had 'flunked' Family Week!" He assured me I had not flunked, but because he could see I was terrified about going home, he added, "No pass."

That was a relief, but then I began to give it more thought. If things at home did not go well, I could bring it up in our meeting on Monday and receive advice on how to handle it. So I returned to him and asked for a pass. He gave it, and I went in search of the Sisters. When I informed Sister Francis Clare that I could return to the monastery for a day, she was shocked. She said that she wanted to have time to share with the community what she had learned about alcoholism before I returned. So I gave the pass back to the counselor. A patient who was going home that day witnessed this and asked if she and her husband could pick me up on Sunday after Mass and take me to lunch and on a sightseeing tour of Baton Rouge. The counselor gave permission. I felt very grateful and stayed in touch with her for sometime afterwards.

During the final weeks of treatment, we were given a guide to the 4th step: "(We) made a searching and fearless moral inventory of ourselves." Each page listed a character defect on one side and a virtue on the other. The inventory was to be written seriously and quietly. If we needed help, we could ask for it, but we were to show what we were writing to no one. I was also told to write ten good attributes about myself—ones I could honestly claim. With one small light over the recessed desk so it wouldn't keep my two roommates awake, I wrestled with that until 2:00

A.M. I had written down two. Usually one is advised to destroy the inventory after one makes a 5th step (mandatory back then in many treatment centers), but no one suggested I do that. So I kept mine. For the most part, I had a clear view of negatives and weaknesses, but I could claim only a couple of positive attributes.

When the inventory was completed, we were assigned a day, time, and person with whom to share it. Usually the person who listened to a 4th step inventory was a member of the clergy or a person familiar with the 5th step: "(We) admitted to God (always in terms of a personal belief of how to define God or a higher power greater than oneself), to ourselves, and to another human being the exact nature of our wrongs." The higher power can be nature, an AA group or some other power in one's life—even a doorknob (What does a doorknob do?), but never one human being. Steps 4 and 5 are unique in that they are the only steps that may be done only once if one so chooses. The other ten are to be woven into the fabric of one's life.

Since I was a Catholic nun, I expected to have a Priest hear my 5th step. I had observed one coming in to the treatment center. Instead, my counselor informed me that I would do mine with Nathan, the Baptist Chaplain. My heart sank. What would he think of a Catholic nun who was an alcoholic and had a story like mine?

I kept close to what was written in the guide and answered his questions as truthfully as I could, but I kept my eyes on the guidebook—afraid and ashamed to look at him. At the end I looked up, expecting to see condemnation in his face. To my shock, I saw kindness and compassion. I could not believe it. I was overcome and thought, "Nathan likes me!" I couldn't fathom it. He took my 4th step guide and wrote a few sentences of advice and encouragement (another reason I never destroyed it). It was the beginning of a healing process.

The next step was to give a short farewell to our fellow patients. After that a former patient came to take me to the bus depot. I boarded a bus to New Orleans for an overnight stay before I left the following morning for a halfway house in Omaha, Nebraska. My counselor had recommended to me that before I returned to monastic life, I spend three months in a halfway house for women alcoholics. Because it bore a saint's name, he thought other Sisters had spent time there. No other Sister had. The reason he gave me for the recommendation was my fear of returning home. I believe he also was afraid I might return to drinking.

My recollection of the evening I arrived in New Orleans remains blurred. One of the Sisters picked me up at the bus depot and took me to the monastery. I have only one memory of that evening. My closest friend, Sister Elizabeth, was the one who carried the wine and the hosts to the altar during Mass that week. She asked me if I'd like to accompany her the next morning and carry the bread or the wine. Seeing it as a symbolic act, I chose the wine.

Shortly after Mass I had to catch a flight to Omaha. I had packed my suitcase with heavier clothes and was ready to leave when Sister Francis Clare summoned me to her office. With her stood Elizabeth and a couple of other Sisters. I was accused of drinking. I was shocked; it was the last thing I wanted to do. After Elizabeth said, "Katie, I could smell it on you at Mass." I was in a state of disbelief and protested, "I swear I haven't been drinking!" After that I can't recall saying anything. I shut down inside. A short time later, I was on my way to the airport. I had to change planes in St. Louis. It was a blessing as I became ill with vomiting and diarrhea. Later that afternoon, a teenage girl from Baton Rouge who had been in Omaha for a few weeks and her companion met me at the airport. They took me to the halfway house where I had agreed to stay for three months. Five months later in May 1980, I left.

ೂ

Later when I became a certified chemical dependency counselor, I learned what a healthy halfway house should be. The one in Omaha was not typical. We were repeatedly told: "Winners don't come to halfway houses." Meetings usually consisted of hot seat confrontations. Shortly after I left in May, I discovered I had been kept for two extra months and made house manager because the census was at a low point.

A few positive things happened. After the initial month, we had to pay our own room and board. As soon as I could leave the house to look for work, I applied at as many places as possible, even at a kiosk in a department store. I knew that my work hours had to leave me free to be in the house for group sessions in the early evening. After my years in the cloister, I didn't have many marketable skills. However, in the monastery, I had cared for the sick for several years with success even while drinking. So I answered an ad in the Sunday paper for a class for nursing assistants at Bergen Mercy Hospital. It began immediately. Upon completion of the course, I was hired there to work from 11:00 P.M. to 7:00 A.M. The orthopedic doctor I was seeing told me I could not lift patients because of my back, but I needed the job. In May, when I left the halfway house, I suffered a severe stress fracture and soon had to leave the hospital work.

ೂ

Two events occurred shortly after I left the halfway house. The 45th Annual Convention of Alcoholics Anonymous was held in New Orleans and my leave-of-absence was up. I returned to a grateful celebration of my eight months of sobriety. During the AA Convention I stayed at Fara's convent and rode each day with my doctor's wife to the Super Dome where it was held.

Lois Wilson, the widow of Bill Wilson, co-founder of Alcoholics Anonymous, was present at the convention. On the final evening, she was to be presented with the first Italian translation of The Big Book by a representative from Italy. The flags of all the nations represented at the convention were to be flown. Alas, my doctor's wife thought I had made other arrangements for transportation that evening and failed to pick me up. There was no way I could miss this last evening of such an important event in my new sobriety, so I boarded a city bus that ran in front of Fara's convent.

I asked the driver where I could transfer to the special bus for the Super Dome. She noticed my small white tag, which featured jazz stick men and in small letters read "the Forty-fifth Annual Convention of Alcoholics Anonymous." She immediately asked, "Say, who are all you people running around with those little white badges?" I replied that most of us were from Alcoholics Anonymous but that a large number were from Al-Anon. Immediately, she turned to the other occupants of the bus and in a loud voice asked, "Did y'all hear that? Those people running around wearing little white tags are former drunks!" Then she said, "Lady, You've got your problem licked." Immediately, the riders on the bus began an animated discussion on how to avoid problems with alcohol, which included eating a stick of butter before going out to drink. I sat there, embarrassed and amused. Fortunately I met the right bus and arrived at the convention in time to meet our small group from Omaha and tell them about my experience. They urged me to get down on the stage and share my newfound knowledge with the assembly. What an event for someone newly sober!

The following day I went to the monastery for an appointment with Sister Francis Clare. I had been advised to ask for an extension of my leave of absence while I prayed and sought direction about my future. In light of the way my life at the monastery in New Orleans would be under constant surveillance, I knew I could not return there. I was met by Sister Francis Clare and her whole Council. She told me she knew I would ask for more time and the answer was "No." I had to return immediately or write for a dispensation from my vows, the last thing I wanted to do.

The discussion about my future was negative and I left. (Here I need to say that the Sisters only knew the negative facts about active alcoholism and nothing of the positive possibilities of a healthy recovery program.) At that time I was devastated. As elderly Jesuit friend picked me up that afternoon to take me to the airport where I was scheduled to fly back to Omaha. I was nearly hysterical with grief. He kept reassuring me that I would never give up my vows in my heart— that this was only a legal choice. It did not assuage my grief.

❧

Back in Omaha, I had to find work and decide what to do. The day after returning, my leg that had had the stress fracture, became painful and swollen. This was due to the walking I had done during the Convention. The doctor ordered me to keep it elevated for several days—no standing or walking. One of the Poor Clares took me to buy food and left me comfortably seated in my apartment.

In view of the fact that I was a qualified nursing assistant, I called a company who hired nurses and assistants to care for people in their homes. I was accepted. As soon as my leg healed, I was sent to a home in a beautiful section of Omaha to care for the elderly parents of the homeowner whose husband was dying of cancer. The younger couple owned an exclusive store for women's clothing. They already had another nursing assistant who was caring for the husband. My duties were light. I arrived at noon Monday through Friday, took their vital signs, and prepared lunch. While they napped, I cleaned or washed clothes, prepared supper, and left when their daughter returned home. I grew to love them, but I knew I'd have to find a better paying job eventually. A couple of mornings each week I recorded magazine articles for the blind for Nebraska Public Radio. Their studio was walking distance from my apartment. Since my mornings were free, I felt a sense of purpose in this.

Another important bright spot in my life that summer was my relationship with a woman who had become my sponsor in A.A. after I left the halfway house. Although she was tall and slender, her name was "Chubby." She and her husband, who was running for another term as Nebraska State Senator, were both in Alcoholics Anonymous. Their large home was open to me at all times. It was a healing atmosphere. We had met during the latter part of my stay in the halfway house when a young woman resident took me to a large Sunday morning meeting at an A.A. Club in Council Bluffs, Iowa. We were too numerous to have an opportunity for everyone to speak at the meeting. Thus, each Sunday the leader stopped ten minutes or so before the hour was up and asked if anyone not called on needed to speak. If no one indicated a need to share, the leader looked at this woman and asked, "Chubby, speak to us about gratitude?" I knew I wanted her for my sponsor. Our relationship continued after I left Omaha until her death.

❧

The days went by. I could not write to Rome requesting a dispensation from my vows. The Provincial of the Sisters of St. Joseph in St. Paul was waiting for me to move the process along, but I could not do it. Then my beloved Fara, who was Vicar of Religious in New Orleans, called me and informed me that she had received the necessary papers from the New Orleans monastery and was waiting on my letter. On the Feast of St. Clare, I was off work and I determined that I was going nowhere that day until I wrote and mailed the request for dispensation to Fara. I cannot describe my feelings. Everything in me fought against it, but I knew I could not return to New Orleans. Fara called and asked permission to share my letter with Sister Francis Clare. I truly did not know what I had written. I said "No." The letter was on its way to Rome.

I called Sister Kathleen Marie, Provincial of the Sisters of St. Joseph in St. Paul, to give her the information. In view of what had happened previously, she informed me she could not begin the process of my entry into the "C.S.J.'s." I had to see the "Mother General" in St. Louis. In a few days, the Mother General could see me in the St. Louis airport as she was leaving for a period of time. A day or so before that the husband of the woman whose parents I was caring for died, and Shiva was set for the evening of my trip to St. Louis. His wife asked me to return in time to help with that.

In the morning I flew to St. Louis. Sister Kathleen Marie had described the Mother General to me so well that although several people were moving about under the "Spirit of St. Louis," I recognized her immediately and went to meet her. We met over coffee. She asked me several questions. I remember only one: "Since you are not drinking now, how are you coping with life?" I simply replied "With Alcoholics Anonymous." Our visit was short. She told me she needed time to reflect on it and would let me know her decision through Sister Kathleen Marie in not more than two weeks.

Late that afternoon, as I thought about our conversation, I was amazed at the deep peace that filled my soul. I had an unshakable faith that God was caring for me. I had done what I could do. I left the outcome in God's hands—whatever it might be. Back in Omaha that evening, I had the privilege of helping with Shiva.

A few days later I lost my job. The company called me to say that the woman who had hired me now had to run the clothing store alone. This meant she would periodically leave Omaha on buying trips to New York. A caretaker was needed who could drive her parents to appointments in her absence. Ninety-three-year-old Aaron was weeping about my leaving them. I knew I would miss him and his wife.

The following Sunday, I saw an ad in the help-wanted section for a proofreader in a law firm, a position I had never considered. Immediately I decided to respond. The next day I went downtown to the office and took the grammar and punctuation test and made no mistakes, so they arranged for me to go the law firm on the following day with the admonition that I "dress nicely" because it was a "prestigious firm." I can't remember what I wore; my wardrobe was very limited. Another test was given there, and I was hired. Two days later another proofreader was also hired, a beautiful twenty-five year old former high school teacher named

Connie. There were nine of us—everyone but me was either a former teacher or a college student working to earn tuition. We all liked each other. Connie and I became close friends—going to talks at nearby Creighton University or a movie together. After work on Friday, we often went to supper as a group and then to someone's home to play games. It gave me a social life that as a Sister looking for community I could not otherwise have had. (After my return to St. Paul, Connie came to visit every fall, eventually coming with her husband until her death from cancer when she was forty-six years old.)

☙

Two weeks after my visit to St. Louis, word came that my entrance into the Sisters of St. Joseph in St. Paul had been approved. Six weeks later my dispensation from my vows arrived. I had to sign it in front of a witness. Connie took me to the Poor Clares where I asked Sister Eunice, the former Abbess of the Federation, to witness it. She begged me to transfer to their small community in Omaha instead of going through with the dispensation, but I couldn't do it. However, I shall never forget her support when I was Coordinator of the Program at St. Teresa's and her kindness to me through the years. The following Saturday, Sister Kathleen Marie and her companion, Sister Marie, came to Omaha. In a simple ceremony before the icon in my apartment, they welcomed me to the first step on my journey to become a Sister of St. Joseph in the St. Paul Province.

On Christmas Eve I journeyed to St. Paul by bus to spend time with the small group of Sisters I expected to live with later in the spring after my year of living on my own in Omaha had ended. In the middle of April, I left the law firm where they held a surprise farewell party for me. I took the bus to Massachusetts to spend a week at a residential treatment center for priests and nuns, as my goal, at that time, was to work with alcoholic Sisters. I stayed in a small house down the road from the center with one of the counselors and attended everything except the small groups with the patients. I learned later that an Irish priest from California had initially believed I was a "plant" and had warned others to be wary of me. After a couple of days that changed and everyone became very friendly. At the end of the week I flew to St. Paul where Sister Marie and another Sister met me at the airport.

To my disappointment I learned that due to unforeseen circumstances, I should not be living with the small group with whom I previously stayed. Instead, I should join three others who were forming a small community. I didn't know any of them. At the time I needed an established group and this did not work out. Within two weeks I was living in a parish convent in which Sister Kathleen Marie also lived, and working with Sister Marie de Paul in spiritual care at Bethany, a home for old, retired, and convalescing Sisters. Sister Marie de Paul, the Sister

Administrator, and the Sister Coordinator were welcoming. I enjoyed being there and getting to know many of the Sisters who lived there.

It is difficult to write about that summer. I was often lonely. Feeling the need for an A.A. connection, I telephoned the A.A. Intergroup of the Twin Cities' and asked for a volunteer to take me to a meeting. In half an hour a woman called and later that day picked me up. With her, I attended a meeting, which was close enough for me to walk over from either Bethany or the convent.

C3

Sister Kathleen Marie was a joyful presence when she was at home, but in her position as Provincial, she often had to be absent. In August, I was interviewed by those in leadership and their Council and accepted for entrance into a formal canonical year. At that time I was fifty-eight years old and had been in religious life for forty years. My becoming formally a novice caused a problem as some thought they would have to become a "novitiate house." It was a painful time. I was becoming depressed. My emotional situation became a concern to the two Sisters in charge at Bethany and to Sister Marie de Paul who reached out to me. I eventually confided in Sister Marie de Paul as she had lived in that convent until the previous May. She convinced my Sister companion it was not a good place for me to be. On October 15, I moved to our Provincial House. As Sister Marie and I entered the large dining room at noon, all of the Sisters arose from their chairs, smiled, and said "Welcome, Catherine!" I was at home.

Bethany, where I continued to work with Sister Marie de Paul, was next to the Provincial House. Two or three times each week, I took the bus to the novitiate to study the history of our community with our two young novices, and social justice classes with them and young women from a couple of other communities. As most of the Sisters I lived with were my age and older, that was interesting, a foot in the worlds of older and younger women.

After thirty-six years, I cannot remember how I met a woman who had started the Ramsey County Senior Citizen Program for alcoholic seniors. I asked her to be my sponsor and began to attend senior meetings on a regular basis. I have no doubt that she would have given her life for a suffering alcoholic, but her expectations began to cause some problems in my life as a woman religious because I also had obligations as a community member. I consulted Father Arnie Luger, a recovering alcoholic Priest who was active in A.A. and in Calix (a group of recovering Catholics whose members not only attended regular A.A. meetings, but also met once a month for Mass, Communion, and a breakfast together, followed by a speaker). Father was kind, gentle, and active in the recovery community. Many people esteemed him. He strongly advised me that except for faithful attendance at Alcoholics Anonymous meetings, my community obligations came first. He had known and respected my sponsor for a long time but told me I had to break the sponsor relationship. That was very difficult but I agreed it was necessary.

One of my finest memories of that year was my introduction to Sister Marie Philip, who lived at the Provincial House after her retirement from many years heading the French Department at the College of St. Catherine. In between, she had spent several years at our House of Prayer in Stillwater. Two or three times each week I met with her to learn the Maxims of Jean Pierre Medaille, S. J., the Jesuit who (along with six women) founded our community in France in the seventeenth century. Sisters my age had had to memorize all one hundred maxims when they were in the novitiate. Sister Marie Philip suggested we read them and choose two or three to pray over and then discuss when we met. We shared intimately, and soon became loving friends. She was extremely intelligent but also was one of the most loving and caring women I have ever known. Our relationship continued until her death in 1996.

Life in the Provincial House was good. I made several friends there and in A.A.. Then, the following summer, our Provincial and Council changed. I looked forward to becoming a vowed member of the community in October 1982. In August I met with Sister Karen Kennelly and the individual members of her council and was accepted for vows. I had assumed vows would be for a period of three years and then the possibility of final vows. To my astonishment, I was offered a choice: temporary vows or perpetual vows! I was literally dumbfounded, but I had no doubt, which I longed for and chose "final vows." Later that day the call came: final profession on October 15. The Sisters at the Provincial House rejoiced with me. The next two months were spent in ardent preparation and in a directed eight-day retreat at our House of Prayer in Stillwater, Minnesota.

During this period I was also looking for a ministry with and to chemically dependent persons. To that end I took classes wherever they were offered, both those informative about chemical dependency and those directly spiritual including a class in the hearing of 5th steps given by Dr. Ed Selner at St. Catherine's. I also took two excellent classes in human sexuality: one at the University of Minnesota and the other called "Sexual Should's and Where They Come From" at St Catherine's.

On October 15, 1982, I pronounced my perpetual vows of poverty, chastity, and obedience. This occurred during evening Mass celebrated by my friend, Father Arnie Luger, and surrounded by people I loved--family members and Sisters of St. Joseph, and Poor Clares from Bloomington.

◳

My friend, and at the time still my sponsor in Alcoholics Anonymous, invited me to work in the Ramsey County program for seniors at Mounds Park Hospital in St. Paul. I would be subsidized by the Urban League for six months. I thought I'd be working with the seniors in the program and hearing 5th steps. However, her plan was that I would make 12-step calls on seniors, especially those still drinking. Disappointed, I went with her to meet Duane Bertelson, the Director of the chemical dependency program. When he learned that I had taken a class in hearing 5th steps, he immediately asked me if I'd be willing to work with Reverend Roy Gardner, the chaplain, who was overburdened with being both chaplain and the counselor for the seniors in the program. I was overjoyed. (Reverend Roy Gardner and his wife, Shirley, became good friends and have remained so to this day.)

I loved my ministry at Mounds Park Hospital. The nurses and counselors in the chemical dependency unit liked and supported one another. Our Provincial House continued to be a good place to live. My duties there fit into my new schedule. It was a peaceful place to be. Later, I presided over the Sunday Service at Mounds once a month.

Shortly after that, Father Luger suggested to Father Mark Mindrup, O. F. M. Conventual, who had started A.A. and Al-Anon retreats at the Franciscan Retreat House in Prior Lake, that he invite me to be a speaker during the retreat. In 1988 after one of the Friars was missioned to Mississippi, I became a member of the retreat team. I loved going out there and meeting other recovering people, sharing with them, the Friars on the team, and other priests who gave conferences. This lasted until the format changed. I left in 1999 to engage in women's retreats, including one for women religious, as well as to hear 5th steps for many years. My life was full. In our Community I joined the Justice Commission and the Membership Committee.

In 1987, Mounds Park Hospital was closed, the smallest and first of the Health East Hospitals to close. As I had received a scholarship to Rutgers Summer School of Alcohol Studies for the month of July, I said goodbye to my friends there. At the end of August, the place closed. The following October, we had a formal closing. I was asked to lead a prayer and I thought, "In 1905, when this Baptist Hospital opened, a Catholic nun would never have been asked to take part in a prayer service. If she had, she would not have received permission to do so." To this day, thirty years later, some of us who worked there still get together.

In August of that year, I was invited to become part of the staff at our House of Prayer in Stillwater. I happily accepted. Then the Sisters realized I was supposed to have asked to be a member of the staff, and a decision would need to be made. To adhere to protocol, I asked, they said "Yes." I moved out there after my return from Rutgers.

I grew to love Stillwater. Our House of Prayer, a convent, was a peaceful place to be. Three of us who had formal training in spiritual direction engaged in direction and retreats and two of us for several months heard 5th steps in the chemical dependency treatment program sponsored by Health East. Then it was decided to have my friend, Reverend Roy Gardner who was the Chaplain in chemical dependency at St. Joseph's Hospital, cover Stillwater as well. I was undecided about what to do. I loved the House of Prayer, but I missed my connection with a chemical dependency program, both lecturing and hearing 5th steps with people with whom I could so closely relate. That decision was settled for me in August of 1988 when the new Pastor decided to take the House of Prayer for parish offices, and we Sisters returned to St. Paul.

I soon had my own office, first at the St. Paul Area Council of Churches, and then at our own Carondelet Center where I continued to hear 5th steps and to engage for a while in spiritual direction. After a couple of years, I discovered I was more comfortable engaging with persons in 12-step programs, so I gave up direction with others and worked with members of Alcoholics Anonymous, Al-Anon, and Emotions Anonymous.

☙

Influenced by Chubby, my first sponsor, and by the fact that I began a sober life on the eve of Thanksgiving, I was filled with gratitude for the gift of sobriety and a desire to share it with others. To that end, I took classes wherever I could find them on spirituality and sexuality. The College of St. Catherine (now St. Catherine University) even offered a course in the hearing of 5th steps, one of the most difficult but healing steps of the 12-step program of Alcoholics Anonymous. Two months after my final profession of vows as a Sister of St. Joseph, I began what I considered an unofficial "internship," funded by the Urban League, at Mounds Park Hospital in St. Paul. Six months later I was hired as a chaplain counselor with the stipulation that I become certified as a counselor. As I have noted before, it was a wonderful place to work.

At that time I also tried small group living, a great change from living at the Provincial House. At first I was too idealistic. After a couple of years, I returned to the Provincial House. (In later years a Sister from that small group and I became "soul Sisters," able to share spiritually on a very deep level until her death in 2009.) After a time at the Provincial House, I was ready to try small group living again—this time with more realistic expectations. Four years later, I could no longer manage the stairs in our Victorian house. I received permission to live in an apartment and to enjoy the quiet time I needed.

Meanwhile, my ministry of retreat work continued. I heard 5th steps and lectured at various places. During that time, 1989–1994, I was also able to be involved in AIDS ministry for the Archdiocese of St. Paul-Minneapolis. From 1998 through 2006, another Sister and I became members of Prisoner Visitation and Support and visited "our guys" in Sandstone State Prison. Ill health ended that for both of us.

ଓ

I have especially loved working with alcoholics in recovery. I felt truly blessed to be able to use my recovery to help others even as I continued to be helped by other members of Alcoholics Anonymous, especially those in our group whose insights continue to enrich me.

Into my eighties, I was able to continue hearing 5th steps, but eventually I realized that my energy level was decreasing. I learned to "let go and let God." Now, I simply attend Alcoholics Anonymous meetings and have the joy of welcoming young women and men and other newcomers into our group. Even that exertion is sometimes too much now, but I am filled with gratitude for the gift of sobriety, the gift of faithful and loving friends in my two religious communities—in the recovery community and among other people who have come into my life in other ways and continue to enrich it.

Recovery has blessed me in untold ways.

Glossary

Apostolic: Engaged in active ministry.

Anointed: Received the sacrament of the Anointing of the Sick. See James 5.14-15.

Breviary: Book of prayer, mostly psalms and readings from scripture. Prayed daily by many nuns and priests.

CSJ: Congregation of Saint Joseph.

Extern: A sister who does not live exclusively within the enclosure and goes on outside errands.

Men or Women Religious: This is a term used by the Catholic Church for people who belong to a community under a chosen or designated leader, for example, Franciscans, Benedictines, and Poor Clares. Often they live together. Frequently now, men or women religious live near or at their places of ministry and gather together at designated times for meetings, religious observations, or other activity.

Novice: After a trial period of six months to a year, a novice tended to leave or was asked to be accepted as a member of the religious community. As a member, she received a habit, the special attire of the particular community she was joining. She was also given a new name. Often she wore a white veil to distinguish her from the vowed members. At the present time, many community members wear modern clothing and do not wear veils.

Postulant: This title, although not currently prevalent, refers to one who enters a religious community. The period of time a person is a postulant usually lasts for a period of six months to a year. One may leave at any time.

Acknowledgments

First of all, I want to acknowledge my "soul sister" Anne Godine, CSJ. She persisted in asking me over and over through a period of several years, "When are you going to write your memoirs?" Anne had already left for eternity when I began. Then there were several members of our Alcoholics Anonymous group who continued to encourage me and hold me accountable.

When I finally began, my dear friend JoAnn Hillstrom offered to type my handwritten pages for me. She has faithfully done this during these past several years. Margaret Hasse, a published poet and teacher of writing in the Twin Cities, has read and given feedback to my work as I went along. Her questions about Catholic religious life have proved extremely helpful. Initially, I took too much for granted about reader knowledge of terms common in religious life, especially in former years.

I want to acknowledge my physicians, Bradley Langley, M.D., who has been my doctor and friend for over thirty years, and Andrew Portis, M.D., my kidney doctor who has kept his promise to do everything in his power to make it possible for me to finish.

For these friends and for everyone else who has encouraged me along the way, I am grateful. I could not have done it without you. Ansgar Holmberg created a beautiful cover and also sat and listened to my raspy voice for four hours, one hour each day, for a final proofreading and made helpful comments.

I fervently hope my story will help other women who hide their illness in shame, as I did for many years, to get help and live full and happy lives.

To the Sisters of St. Joseph who accepted me as a member of their community in 1980 (and finally in 1982), I am truly grateful.

Catherine Jenkins, CSJ

About the Author

Catherine Jenkins was born on June 7, 1923, in St. Paul, Minnesota, to Loren Thomas and Anne Connelly Jenkins. She was a student in St. Paul public and parochial schools. After high school graduation at age eighteen, Catherine entered the Poor Clare Monastery, a contemplative community, in Sauk Rapids, Minnesota. In 1953, Sister Catherine was one of six Sisters who founded a Poor Clare Monastery in Bloomington, Minnesota. As Vicaress, an assistant to the Abbess, she had access to wine and brandy that were given by benefactors. Sister Catherine became an alcoholic at age thirty-five, but her drinking was hidden until 1979 when, at age fifty-six, she was sent to a treatment program in Baton Rouge, Lousisiana.

Her B.A. in theology from St. Teresa College, Winona, Minnesota, 1975, was followed by further graduate studies in theology from Xavier University and Loyola University in New Orleans, Louisiana, and Saint Bonaventure University in Allegany, New York. In 1980, she transferred to the Sisters of St. Joseph of Carondelet, in St. Paul, Minnesota. Sister Catherine worked as a chaplain and chemical dependency counselor and as an initiator and speaker at retreats primarily for women. From 1989-1994, Sister Catherine worked for the local archdiocesan AIDS program as a visitor to those suffering with the disease. She began writing her memoir in 2012.